Story and Illustrations by Nancy Passman
Copyright© 2022

ISBN 979-8-218-11991-1

"We do not like all of you bossy
upper case letters telling us what to do.
WE QUIT!" announced lower case **a**.

Upper case **A** answered,
"You are small and we are tall,
so we tell you what to do,
and quitting is **not** going to happen."

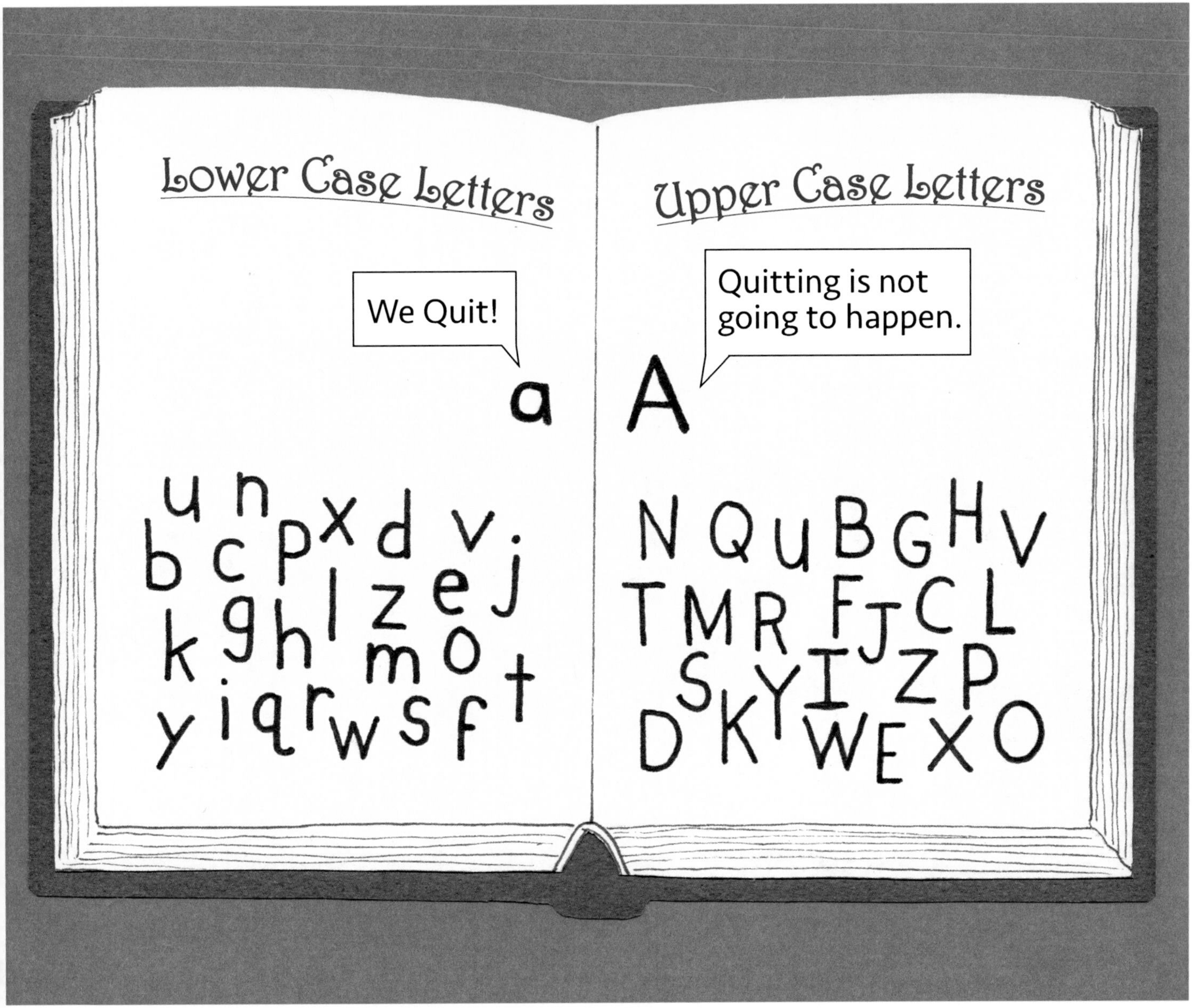
Lower Case Letters
Upper Case Letters
We Quit!
a
A
Quitting is not going to happen.

But it did happen.

That night the lower case letters quit and ran away.

They piled into a treasure chest that could float like a boat, then began to drift away... far, far away.

And when their boat stopped with a jolt,
they all climbed out and took their first step
onto Banana Island.

The lowercase letters felt free at last!
They babbled like babies
and wandered wherever they wanted.

They knew nothing about living in the **real** world.
For example, the entire alphabet went and
walked right off a cliff!

a was leading the way
when the alphabet came upon two paths.
Every letter took the one less traveled
and **that** made all the difference.

Because of a bumble bee
b bumped into a boulder.

c chanted, "Catch me if you can!"
to curious creatures.

Dancing down the dunes
d discovers a dog.

e enjoys eating everything.

f flees from the forest in a frenzy,

then flips and falls.

g giggles and gets googly eyes.

A hat help **h** hide from the heat.

Lower case **i**
has a dot like an eye.

j jingle jangles in the jungle.

A crown is found in a cave by **k**.

Listen to **l** yell.

In the morning **m** meets many monkeys.

Nearby native noise makes **n** nervous.

Next to **n** is **o**.

Put together, they spell no.

p parachutes past private places.

q is courted by the king.

r realizes the risk of roaming in the rainforest.

At the sight of civilization
s sighed and said "Sweet."

t trekked on the trail on top of a tiger's tail.

u utters an insult to **n**.

v voices a viewpoint... not knowing that
a visit to a volcano is a very bad idea.

w wonders and worries.

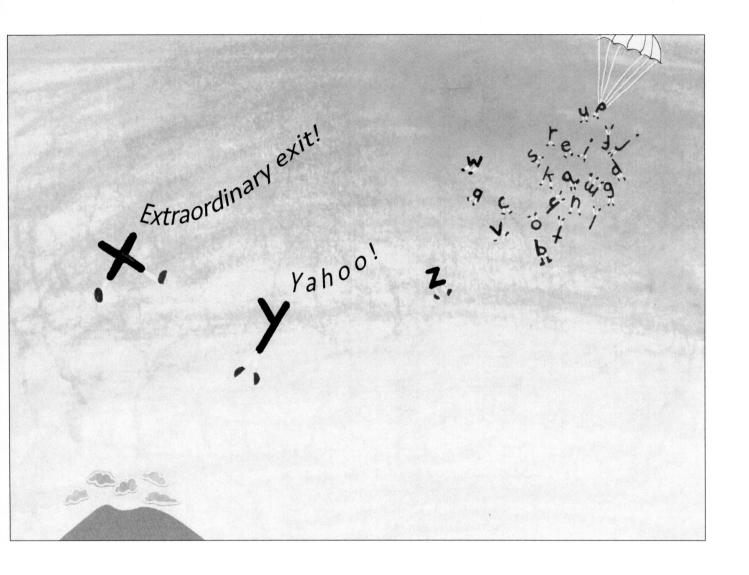

Then without warning the wind went *WHOOSH.*

"Extraordinary exit!" exclaimed **x.**

"Yahoo!" yelled **y.**

The entire alphabet was whisked up to a bed of clouds.
Dizzy and dumbstruck, they all soon fell fast asleep...
except for **z**.

It was **not** a good morning for the runaway alphabet.
They were stuck inside a dark, damp, raincloud.
And when it burst open
all 26 letters tumbled back down to Banana Island,

where with a plip and sometimes a plop,
they all ended up in a big black pot
and became soup.

And all who tasted it said, "Mmm mmm good."

Aa Bb Cc Dd

Ee Ff Gg

Hh Ii Jj Kk

Ll Mm Nn Oo Pp

Qq Rr Ss

Tt Uu Vv

Ww Xx Yy Zz

Made in United States
North Haven, CT
21 January 2023

31424138R00022